Healing Flowers: Bach Flower Remedies Guided Meditations

Goutham Krishnadas

Copyright

Table of Contents

Introduction: Understanding Bach Flower Remedies and Guided Meditation Practice

Welcome to a transformative journey of self-discovery and emotional healing with Bach Flower remedies. We will explore the essence of Bach Flower remedies and how guided meditations can be used as a powerful tool to harness their healing potential.

What are Bach Flower Remedies?

Bach Flower remedies are a gentle yet profound system of natural healing developed by Dr. Edward Bach in the early 20th century. Dr. Bach believed that emotional imbalances lie at the root of physical illness and sought to address these imbalances with the use of plant-based essences. Each of the 38 Bach Flower remedies is derived from a specific wildflower or plant and is uniquely suited to address a particular emotional state or personality trait.

How do Bach Flower Remedies Work?

Bach Flower remedies work by addressing the underlying emotional patterns and imbalances that contribute to physical and mental distress. These remedies help to restore harmony and balance to the emotional body, allowing for greater well-being and vitality. Bach Flower essences are safe, non-toxic, and gentle enough to be used by people of all ages, including children and pets.

Using Guided Meditations with Bach Flower Remedies

Guided meditations offer a powerful way to deepen our connection with Bach Flower remedies and integrate their healing properties into our lives. In these guided meditations, we will explore the energetic qualities of each Bach Flower remedy and invite participants to connect with their healing essence on a deep and transformative level.

How to Use These Guided Meditations

To fully benefit from these guided meditations, find a quiet and comfortable space where you can relax without interruption. Set aside dedicated time for your meditation practice, ideally at a time when you can fully immerse yourself in the experience. Follow along with the guided meditation, allowing yourself to surrender to the process and open your heart to the healing energy of the Bach Flower remedy being explored.

Intention Setting

Before beginning each guided meditation, take a moment to set an intention for your practice. Reflect on the emotional state or aspect of yourself that you would like to work with, and invite the healing energy of the Bach Flower remedy to support you on your journey. Trust in the wisdom of your inner guidance and allow yourself to receive the insights and healing that arise during the meditation.

Closing Reflection

At the end of each guided meditation, take a few moments to reflect on your experience. Notice any shifts or insights that may have emerged during the meditation and honor the healing work that you have done. Express gratitude for the support of the Bach Flower remedy and the guidance of the meditation, knowing that you are supported on your journey of healing and self-discovery.

Overview of 38 Bach Flower Meditations

Chapter 1: Bach Flower Agrimony

This essence, renowned for its capacity to aid individuals who conceal their inner turmoil behind a veneer of cheerfulness, becomes our focal point. As we engage in guided meditation, we are guided to peel back the layers of pretense, embracing vulnerability and authenticity as pathways to inner peace.

Chapter 2: Bach Flower Aspen

Selected for its prowess in assuaging nebulous fears and uncertainties, Aspen beckons us to relinquish control and trust in the unseen currents of existence. Through guided meditation, we navigate the realm of courage, finding solace in embracing the enigmatic nature of life.

Chapter 3: Bach Flower Beech

Revered for its capacity to dissolve judgmental tendencies and nurture empathy, Beech encourages us to foster understanding and unity with all beings. Guided meditation serves as our conduit, facilitating the expansion of our hearts and the cultivation of compassion.

Chapter 4: Bach Flower Centaury

Recognized for its support of individuals struggling to assert their boundaries, Centaury becomes a beacon of self-care and empowerment. Through guided meditation, we honor our needs and reclaim our sovereignty, forging a path toward inner strength and resilience.

Chapter 5: Bach Flower Cerato

Revered for its capacity to quiet the incessant chatter of the mind and amplify our intuitive faculties, Cerato becomes our guiding light towards inner clarity and self-trust. Through the conduit of guided meditation, we embark on a profound journey inward, tapping into the wellspring of our own wisdom and intuition, discovering the answers we seek nestled within the depths of our being.

Chapter 6: Bach Flower Cherry Plum

Renowned for its ability to calm tumultuous emotions and restore inner harmony, Cherry Plum offers sanctuary amidst life's storms. Through guided meditation, we surrender to the tranquil currents of serenity, releasing fear and tension as we embrace the profound sense of balance that resides within us.

Chapter 7: Bach Flower Chestnut Bud

Here, amidst the fertile soil of personal development, we nurture the seeds of growth with Bach Flower Chestnut Bud. Acknowledged for its support in aiding individuals to glean wisdom from past experiences, Chestnut Bud becomes our companion on the journey towards self-awareness and evolution. Through guided meditation, we embark on a transformative odyssey, embracing change and unfurling into the fullness of our potential.

Chapter 8: Bach Flower Chicory

Revered for its capacity to nurture unconditional love and selflessness, Chicory becomes a beacon illuminating the path towards deeper connections and boundless kindness. Through guided meditation, we open the floodgates of our hearts, allowing the gentle currents of love to flow freely, enriching our lives and those around us.

Chapter 9: Bach Flower Clematis

Within this Meditation, we traverse the ethereal realms of Bach Flower Clematis. Celebrated for its ability to awaken creativity and ignite visionary thinking, Clematis inspires us to breathe life into our dreams and aspirations. Through guided meditation, we embark on a voyage of self-discovery, harnessing the power of imagination to transform our visions into tangible reality.

Chapter 10: Bach Flower Crab Apple

Here, in the sacred sanctuary of purification, we cleanse body, mind, and spirit with Bach Flower Crab Apple. Revered for its ability to purge negativity and foster self-acceptance, Crab Apple becomes our ally in the pursuit of inner purity. Through guided meditation, we release the shackles of self-doubt and embrace the radiant essence of our true selves, emerging purified and renewed.

Chapter 11: Bach Flower Elm

Recognized for its ability to bolster confidence and resilience, Elm becomes our ally in navigating moments of overwhelm and self-doubt. Through the transformative practice of guided meditation, we reconnect with the wellspring of our inner strength, summoning the courage to confront life's challenges with steadfast resolve and unwavering determination.

Chapter 12: Bach Flower Gentian

Revered for its capacity to uplift the spirit and restore faith, Gentian offers solace in moments tainted by doubt and disappointment. Guided by the soothing currents of meditation, we cultivate trust in the inherent beauty of life's journey, embracing each twist and turn with an open heart and unwavering optimism.

Chapter 13: Bach Flower Gorse

Celebrated for its ability to infuse optimism and positivity, Gorse beckons us to believe in the transformative power of renewal. Through the gentle guidance of meditation, we awaken the dormant seeds of hope within, illuminating our path with the radiant light of possibility and potential.

Chapter 14: Bach Flower Heather

Known for its ability to promote compassionate listening and understanding, Heather becomes our beacon of connection and harmony. Through the practice of guided meditation, we cultivate the art of deep listening, fostering profound connections and nurturing the bonds of empathy and understanding.

Chapter 15: Bach Flower Holly

Revered for its ability to dissolve barriers and foster compassion, Holly invites us to open our hearts and cultivate empathy for ourselves and others. Guided by the gentle currents of meditation, we release the shackles of negativity, embracing the boundless potential of love to heal and transform our lives.

Chapter 16: Bach Flower Honeysuckle

Celebrated for its ability to release attachments to the past and embrace the magic of the present moment, Honeysuckle invites us to savor the beauty of impermanence. Guided by the gentle whispers of meditation, we release the weight of what no longer serves us, embracing the infinite possibilities that lie ahead.

Chapter 17: Bach Flower Hornbeam

Recognized for its ability to restore enthusiasm and vitality, Hornbeam becomes our beacon of energy and renewal. Guided by the gentle rhythms of meditation, we awaken our inner fire, infusing each moment with renewed vigor and passion for life's endless possibilities.

Chapter 18: Bach Flower Impatiens

Celebrated for its ability to soothe impatience and foster patience, Impatiens invites us to slow down and savor life's precious moments. Guided by the tranquil whispers of meditation, we release the grip of tension, embracing the profound peace that arises from within.

Chapter 19: Bach Flower Larch

Revered for its ability to boost confidence and self-esteem, Larch becomes our guide on the journey to self-realization. Through the transformative practice of guided meditation, we embrace our inner worth, stepping boldly into the radiant light of our true potential.

Chapter 20: Bach Flower Mimulus

Celebrated for its ability to soothe fear and instill bravery, Mimulus offers support for navigating life's uncertainties with grace and resilience. Guided by the gentle currents of meditation, we tap into our inner reservoir of strength, shining brightly in the face of adversity.

Chapter 21: Bach Flower Mustard

Recognised for its ability to lift the clouds of despair and restore inner joy, Mustard becomes our beacon of hope and renewal. Guided by the gentle rhythms of meditation, we release the grip of darkness, embracing the radiant light of hope that illuminates our path.

Chapter 22: Bach Flower Oak

Revered for its ability to instill strength and endurance, Oak becomes our pillar of resilience and fortitude. Guided by the gentle currents of meditation, we reconnect with our inner strength, standing firm in our truth and facing life's trials with unwavering resolve.

Chapter 23: Bach Flower Olive

Celebrated for its ability to replenish energy and restore balance, Olive becomes our fountain of renewal and vitality. Guided by the gentle whispers of meditation, we replenish our reserves, embracing the boundless energy and vitality that flow from within.

Chapter 24: Bach Flower Pine

Revered for its ability to release feelings of guilt and self-blame, Pine becomes our beacon of forgiveness and acceptance. Guided by the gentle currents of meditation, we release the grip of self-judgment, embracing the radiant light of self-love that illuminates our path.

Chapter 25: Bach Flower Red Chestnut

Recognized for its ability to calm worry and foster trust, Red Chestnut becomes our sanctuary of tranquility and inner peace. Guided by the gentle rhythms of meditation, we release the grip of anxiety, embracing the profound peace that arises from within.

Chapter 26: Bach Flower Rock Rose

Celebrated for its ability to instill bravery and resilience, Rock Rose becomes our beacon of strength and fortitude. Guided by the gentle currents of meditation, we tap into our inner reservoir of courage, shining brightly in the face of adversity.

Chapter 27: Bach Flower Rock Water

Revered for its ability to promote flexibility and adaptability, Rock Water becomes our guide on the journey to inner peace and harmony. Guided by the gentle rhythms of meditation, we release the grip of rigidity, embracing the fluidity of life's ever-changing currents.

Chapter 28: Bach Flower Scleranthus

Recognized for its ability to restore inner equilibrium and decision-making, Scleranthus becomes our guide on the journey to balance and clarity. Guided by the gentle currents of meditation, we harmonize body, mind, and spirit, finding alignment with our true desires.

Chapter 29: Bach Flower Star of Bethlehem

Celebrated for its ability to soothe emotional wounds and restore inner peace, Star of Bethlehem becomes our sanctuary of renewal and healing. Guided by the gentle rhythms of meditation, we release the grip of past hurts, embracing the profound healing that arises from within.

Chapter 30: Bach Flower Sweet Chestnut

Revered for its ability to offer comfort and hope in times of despair, Sweet Chestnut becomes our beacon of light and renewal. Guided by the gentle whispers of meditation, we release the grip of darkness, embracing the radiant light of hope that illuminates our path.

Chapter 31: Bach Flower Vervain

Recognized for its ability to promote moderation and relaxation, Vervain becomes our guide on the journey to inner peace and harmony. Guided by the gentle currents of meditation, we release the grip of tension, embracing the tranquility of life's ever-flowing currents.

Chapter 32: Bach Flower Vine

Celebrated for its ability to soften rigid attitudes and foster adaptability, Vine becomes our guide on the journey to flexibility and freedom. Guided by the gentle rhythms of meditation, we release the grip of control, embracing the fluidity of life's ever-changing currents.

Chapter 33: Bach Flower Walnut

Revered for its ability to support transitions and protect against outside influences, Walnut becomes our guide on the journey to renewal and transformation. Guided by the gentle whispers of meditation, we release the grip of resistance, embracing the beauty of life's ever-unfolding tapestry.

Chapter 34: Bach Flower Water Violet

Recognized for its ability to promote openness and receptivity, Water Violet becomes our guide on the journey to deeper connections and harmony. Guided by the gentle currents of meditation, we release the grip of isolation, embracing the interconnectedness of all life.

Chapter 35: Bach Flower White Chestnut

Celebrated for its ability to quiet the mind and enhance mental clarity, White Chestnut becomes our sanctuary of peace and inner wisdom. Guided by the gentle rhythms of meditation, we release the grip of confusion, embracing the profound clarity that arises from within.

Chapter 36: Bach Flower Wild Oat

Within the gentle embrace of self-discovery, we cultivate purpose with Bach Flower Wild Oat. Revered for its ability to support clarity and direction in life's journey, Wild Oat becomes our beacon of purpose and fulfillment. Guided by the gentle whispers of meditation, we release the grip of uncertainty, embracing the radiant path that leads to our true calling.

Chapter 37: Bach Flower Wild Rose

Here, amidst the whispers of renewal, we embrace vitality with Bach Flower Wild Rose. Recognized for its ability to restore enthusiasm and zest for life, Wild Rose becomes our guide on the journey to vitality and passion. Guided by the gentle currents of meditation, we release the grip of apathy, embracing the boundless energy and vitality that flow from within.

Chapter 38: Bach Flower Willow

Celebrated for its ability to support resilience and forgiveness, Willow becomes our sanctuary of peace and inner acceptance. Guided by the gentle rhythms of meditation, we release the grip of bitterness, embracing the profound peace that arises from within.

1. Guided Meditation: Embracing Inner Harmony with Bach Flower Agrimony

Agrimony

Begin by finding a comfortable and quiet space where you can sit or lie down without any distractions. Close your eyes gently, and take a few deep breaths, inhaling deeply through your nose and exhaling slowly through your mouth. With each breath, allow yourself to relax more deeply into the present moment.

Now, bring your awareness to the center of your chest, the area of your heart. Imagine a soft, warm light glowing in this space, radiating comfort and peace. Feel this light expanding with each breath, filling your entire being with a sense of tranquility.

As you continue to breathe deeply, visualize yourself standing in a beautiful meadow, surrounded by tall grasses swaying gently in the breeze. The sun is shining brightly overhead, casting a golden glow all around you. Feel the warmth of the sun on your skin, and the gentle caress of the breeze.

In the distance, you notice a vibrant patch of Agrimony flowers swaying gracefully in the wind. These flowers symbolize the Bach Flower Agrimony remedy, which offers support for inner harmony and emotional balance.

With each step you take towards the Agrimony flowers, feel yourself letting go of any tension or worries that you may be carrying. Allow yourself to release the mask of cheerfulness and embrace your true feelings with compassion and acceptance.

As you reach the Agrimony flowers, take a moment to observe their delicate petals and vibrant colors. Notice how they sway effortlessly in the wind, symbolizing the fluidity and grace of emotional expression.

Now, imagine yourself plucking a few of these Agrimony flowers and holding them gently in your hands. With each petal you touch, feel a sense of inner peace and serenity washing over you. Allow the essence of Agrimony to infuse your being, soothing any inner turmoil or anxiety with its gentle healing energy.

Take a few moments to bask in the calming presence of the Agrimony flowers, allowing their essence to nourish your mind, body, and soul.

When you feel ready, slowly bring your awareness back to the present moment. Wiggle your fingers and toes, gently stretch your body, and take a few more deep breaths.

Know that you can return to this inner sanctuary of peace and harmony whenever you need to reconnect with your true self and find balance amidst life's challenges.

When you're ready, you can slowly open your eyes and return to the world around you, carrying the sense of inner harmony and tranquility with you.

2. Guided Meditation: Embracing Inner Courage with Bach Flower Aspen

Aspen

Find a comfortable and quiet space where you can sit or lie down without any distractions. Close your eyes gently, and take a few deep breaths, inhaling deeply through your nose and exhaling slowly through your mouth. With each breath, allow yourself to relax more deeply into the present moment.

Now, bring your awareness to the center of your chest, the area of your heart. Imagine a soft, warm light glowing in this space, radiating comfort and courage. Feel this light expanding with each breath, filling your entire being with a sense of strength and resilience.

As you continue to breathe deeply, visualize yourself standing in a serene forest, surrounded by tall trees reaching towards the sky. The air is crisp and refreshing, and a gentle breeze rustles the leaves above you. Feel the grounding energy of the earth beneath your feet, anchoring you to the present moment.

In the distance, you notice a cluster of Aspen trees standing tall and proud. These trees symbolize the Bach Flower Aspen remedy, which offers support for facing the unknown and finding inner courage.

With each step you take towards the Aspen trees, feel yourself letting go of any fear or uncertainty that may be weighing you down. Allow yourself to release the grip of anxiety and embrace the unknown with curiosity and confidence.

As you reach the Aspen trees, take a moment to observe their slender trunks and shimmering leaves. Notice how they sway gracefully in the breeze, symbolizing the fluidity and resilience of the human spirit.

Now, imagine yourself standing amidst the Aspen trees, feeling their reassuring presence surrounding you. Feel a sense of inner courage and determination welling up within you, like the sturdy roots of the Aspen trees anchoring you to the earth.

With each breath, draw in the strength and courage of the Aspen trees, allowing their essence to infuse your being. Feel any lingering doubts or fears melting away, replaced by a deep sense of trust in yourself and the journey ahead.

Take a few moments to bask in the empowering energy of the Aspen trees, knowing that you are capable of overcoming any challenge that comes your way.

When you feel ready, slowly bring your awareness back to the present moment. Wiggle your fingers and toes, gently stretch your body, and take a few more deep breaths.

Know that you can return to this inner sanctuary of courage and resilience whenever you need to find strength amidst life's uncertainties.

When you're ready, you can slowly open your eyes and return to the world around you, carrying the sense of inner courage and determination with you.

3. Guided Meditation: Cultivating Compassion with Bach Flower Beech

Beech

Find a quiet and comfortable space where you can sit or lie down without any distractions. Close your eyes gently, and take a few deep breaths, inhaling slowly through your nose and exhaling gently through your mouth. With each breath, allow yourself to relax more deeply into the present moment.

Now, bring your awareness to the center of your chest, the area of your heart. Visualize a soft, warm light glowing in this space, radiating kindness and compassion. Feel this light expanding with each breath, enveloping your entire being in a comforting embrace.

As you continue to breathe deeply, imagine yourself standing in a peaceful forest, surrounded by majestic trees and the soothing sounds of nature. Feel the earth beneath your feet, grounding you and connecting you to the natural world around you.

In the distance, you notice a cluster of Beech trees standing tall and proud. These trees symbolize the Bach Flower Beech remedy, which offers support for cultivating tolerance and understanding towards others.

With each step you take towards the Beech trees, feel yourself letting go of any judgments or criticisms that may be clouding your mind. Allow yourself to release the need to judge others and instead embrace a sense of empathy and compassion.

As you reach the Beech trees, take a moment to observe their sturdy trunks and vibrant leaves. Notice how they sway gently in the breeze, symbolizing the interconnectedness of all living beings.

Now, imagine yourself sitting beneath the canopy of the Beech trees, feeling their peaceful presence surrounding you. Allow yourself to open your heart to the beauty and diversity of the world around you.

With each breath, breathe in the essence of Beech, allowing its healing energy to soften your heart and dissolve any barriers to compassion. Feel a sense of warmth and acceptance flowing through you, connecting you to the inherent goodness within yourself and others.

Take a few moments to bask in the nurturing energy of the Beech trees, knowing that you are capable of extending kindness and understanding to all beings.

When you feel ready, slowly bring your awareness back to the present moment. Wiggle your fingers and toes, gently stretch your body, and take a few more deep breaths.

Know that you can return to this inner sanctuary of compassion and acceptance whenever you need to reconnect with your innate goodness.

When you're ready, you can slowly open your eyes and return to the world around you, carrying the sense of compassion and understanding with you.

4. Guided Meditation: Empowering Boundaries with Bach Flower Centaury

Image Attribution: Squale's Centaury (Centaurium littorale) by Anne Burgess
(https://commons.wikimedia.org/wiki/File:Seaside_Centaury_at_nature_reserve_-_geograph.org.uk_-_1541161.jpg), "Seaside Centaury at nature reserve", https://geograph.org.uk_-_1541161, https://creativecommons.org/licenses/by-sa/2.0/legalcode

Centaury

Find a quiet and comfortable space where you can sit or lie down without any distractions. Close your eyes gently, and take a few deep breaths, allowing yourself to settle into a state of relaxation.

As you continue to breathe deeply, bring your awareness to the center of your chest, the area of your heart. Visualize a soft, warm light glowing in this space, radiating strength and self-assurance. Feel this light expanding with each breath, filling your entire being with a sense of empowerment.

Now, imagine yourself standing in a serene meadow, surrounded by wildflowers and bathed in golden sunlight. Feel the earth beneath your feet, grounding you and supporting you as you connect with the natural world around you.

In the distance, you notice a cluster of Centaury flowers blooming gracefully. These flowers symbolize the Bach Flower Centaury remedy, which offers support for establishing healthy boundaries and honoring your own needs.

With each step you take towards the Centaury flowers, feel yourself shedding any feelings of obligation or servitude that may be weighing you down. Allow yourself to release the need to please others at the expense of your own well-being, and instead embrace a sense of self-respect and assertiveness.

As you reach the Centaury flowers, take a moment to observe their delicate petals and vibrant colors. Notice how they stand tall and proud, symbolizing the strength and resilience that comes from honoring your own boundaries.

Now, imagine yourself sitting amidst the Centaury flowers, feeling their supportive energy surrounding you. Allow yourself to reflect on the importance of setting healthy boundaries in your life, and the freedom that comes from asserting your needs with confidence and clarity.

With each breath, breathe in the essence of Centaury, allowing its healing energy to strengthen your resolve and fortify your sense of self-worth. Feel a sense of empowerment coursing through you, reminding you of your inherent value and worthiness.

Take a few moments to bask in the empowering energy of the Centaury flowers, knowing that you have the strength and courage to honor your own needs and establish boundaries that support your well-being.

When you feel ready, slowly bring your awareness back to the present moment. Wiggle your fingers and toes, gently stretch your body, and take a few more deep breaths.

Know that you can return to this inner sanctuary of empowerment whenever you need to reconnect with your inner strength and assertiveness.

When you're ready, you can slowly open your eyes and return to the world around you, carrying the sense of empowerment and self-respect with you.

5. Guided Meditation: Trusting Inner Wisdom with Bach Flower Cerato

Cerato

Find a quiet and comfortable space where you can sit or lie down without any distractions. Close your eyes gently, and take a few deep breaths, allowing yourself to settle into a state of relaxation.

As you continue to breathe deeply, bring your awareness to the center of your chest, the area of your heart. Visualize a soft, glowing light emanating from this space, representing your inner wisdom and intuition. Feel this light expanding with each breath, filling your entire being with a sense of clarity and insight.

Now, imagine yourself standing at the edge of a tranquil forest, surrounded by towering trees and the soothing sounds of nature. Feel the earth beneath your feet, grounding you and connecting you to the wisdom of the natural world.

In the distance, you notice a path winding its way through the trees, inviting you to embark on a journey of self-discovery. With each step you take along this path, feel yourself letting go of any doubts or uncertainties that may be clouding your mind.

As you walk deeper into the forest, allow yourself to release the need for external validation and instead turn inward to connect with your own inner guidance. Trust that you possess the wisdom and insight needed to navigate life's journey with confidence and clarity.

As you continue along the path, you come across a clearing filled with vibrant Cerato flowers blooming brightly. These flowers symbolize the Bach Flower Cerato remedy, which offers support for trusting your own intuition and inner knowing.

Take a moment to sit amongst the Cerato flowers, feeling their supportive energy enveloping you. Allow yourself to open your heart and mind to the wisdom that resides within you, knowing that you have the answers you seek deep within your own being.

With each breath, breathe in the essence of Cerato, allowing its healing energy to awaken your intuition and strengthen your connection to your inner guidance. Feel a sense of clarity and confidence wash over you, empowering you to trust in yourself and your own abilities.

Take a few moments to bask in the nurturing energy of the Cerato flowers, knowing that you are always supported and guided by the wisdom of your own intuition.

When you feel ready, slowly bring your awareness back to the present moment. Wiggle your fingers and toes, gently stretch your body, and take a few more deep breaths.

Know that you can return to this inner sanctuary of wisdom and insight whenever you need to reconnect with your inner guidance.

When you're ready, you can slowly open your eyes and return to the world around you, carrying the sense of clarity and confidence with you.

6. Guided Meditation: Finding Inner Harmony with Bach Flower Cherry Plum

Cherry plum

Find a quiet and comfortable space where you can sit or lie down without any distractions. Close your eyes gently, and take a few deep breaths, allowing yourself to settle into a state of relaxation.

As you continue to breathe deeply, bring your awareness to the center of your chest, the area of your heart. Visualize a soft, warm light glowing in this space, radiating calmness and tranquility. Feel this light expanding with each breath, filling your entire being with a sense of inner peace.

Now, imagine yourself standing on the banks of a gentle stream, surrounded by lush greenery and the soothing sounds of flowing water. Feel the earth beneath your feet, grounding you and connecting you to the natural world.

In the distance, you notice a cluster of Cherry Plum trees blooming with delicate pink blossoms. These trees symbolize the Bach Flower Cherry Plum remedy, which offers support for finding inner harmony and emotional balance.

With each step you take towards the Cherry Plum trees, feel yourself letting go of any feelings of fear or inner turmoil that may be weighing you down. Allow yourself to release the grip of anxiety and embrace a sense of serenity and calmness.

As you reach the Cherry Plum trees, take a moment to observe their graceful branches and fragrant blossoms. Notice how they sway gently in the breeze, symbolizing the ebb and flow of emotions and the beauty of finding balance within.

Now, imagine yourself sitting beneath the canopy of the Cherry Plum trees, feeling their peaceful presence surrounding you. Allow yourself to let go of any worries or doubts that may be clouding your mind, and instead focus on the present moment.

With each breath, breathe in the essence of Cherry Plum, allowing its healing energy to wash over you and soothe any inner turmoil or tension. Feel a sense of calmness and clarity filling your entire being, like the gentle waters of the stream washing away any negativity or stress.

Take a few moments to bask in the nurturing energy of the Cherry Plum trees, knowing that you are always supported and guided towards inner harmony and emotional balance.

When you feel ready, slowly bring your awareness back to the present moment. Wiggle your fingers and toes, gently stretch your body, and take a few more deep breaths.

Know that you can return to this inner sanctuary of peace and tranquility whenever you need to find balance amidst life's challenges.

When you're ready, you can slowly open your eyes and return to the world around you, carrying the sense of inner harmony and emotional balance with you.

7. Guided Meditation: Embracing Growth with Bach Flower Chestnut Bud

Chestnut bud

Find a comfortable and quiet space where you can sit or lie down without any distractions. Close your eyes gently, and take a few deep breaths, allowing yourself to relax into the present moment.

As you continue to breathe deeply, bring your awareness to the center of your chest, the area of your heart. Visualize a soft, warm light glowing in this space, representing the energy of growth and renewal. Feel this light expanding with each breath, filling your entire being with a sense of possibility and potential.

Now, imagine yourself standing in a beautiful garden, surrounded by vibrant flowers and lush foliage. Feel the earth beneath your feet, grounding you and connecting you to the cycle of nature.

In the distance, you notice a Chestnut Bud beginning to unfurl its delicate leaves. This bud symbolizes the Bach Flower Chestnut Bud remedy, which offers support for learning from past experiences and embracing personal growth.

With each step you take towards the Chestnut Bud, feel yourself letting go of any patterns or behaviors that no longer serve you. Allow yourself to release the grip of the past and embrace a sense of curiosity and openness to new experiences.

As you reach the Chestnut Bud, take a moment to observe its beauty and resilience. Notice how it gently unfolds, symbolizing the potential for growth and transformation that lies within each of us.

Now, imagine yourself sitting beside the Chestnut Bud, feeling its supportive energy enveloping you. Allow yourself to reflect on the lessons and insights gained from past experiences, knowing that each one has helped shape you into the person you are today.

With each breath, breathe in the essence of Chestnut Bud, allowing its healing energy to nourish your spirit and encourage personal growth. Feel a sense of renewal and vitality coursing through you, like the life force flowing through the garden around you.

Take a few moments to bask in the nurturing energy of the Chestnut Bud, knowing that you are always supported and guided on your journey of self-discovery and growth.

When you feel ready, slowly bring your awareness back to the present moment. Wiggle your fingers and toes, gently stretch your body, and take a few more deep breaths.

Know that you can return to this inner sanctuary of growth and renewal whenever you need to reconnect with your inner wisdom and embrace new opportunities.

When you're ready, you can slowly open your eyes and return to the world around you, carrying the sense of possibility and potential with you.

8. Guided Meditation: Nurturing Self-Love with Bach Flower Chicory

Chicory

Find a quiet and comfortable space where you can sit or lie down without any distractions. Close your eyes gently, and take a few deep breaths, allowing yourself to settle into a state of relaxation.

As you continue to breathe deeply, bring your awareness to the center of your chest, the area of your heart. Visualize a soft, warm light glowing in this space, representing the energy of love and compassion. Feel this light expanding with each breath, filling your entire being with a sense of warmth and acceptance.

Now, imagine yourself standing in a vast field of beautiful wildflowers, surrounded by the gentle sounds of nature. Feel the earth beneath your feet, grounding you and connecting you to the natural world.

In the distance, you notice a cluster of Chicory flowers blooming with vibrant blue petals. These flowers symbolize the Bach Flower Chicory remedy, which offers support for nurturing self-love and acceptance.

With each step you take towards the Chicory flowers, feel yourself letting go of any feelings of insecurity or inadequacy that may be weighing you down. Allow yourself to release the need for external validation and instead embrace a sense of unconditional love and self-compassion.

As you reach the Chicory flowers, take a moment to observe their beauty and grace. Notice how they stand tall and proud, symbolizing the strength and resilience that comes from loving oneself unconditionally.

Now, imagine yourself sitting amidst the Chicory flowers, feeling their supportive energy surrounding you. Allow yourself to open your heart to the love and acceptance that resides within you, knowing that you are worthy of love just as you are.

With each breath, breathe in the essence of Chicory, allowing its healing energy to fill you with a deep sense of self-love and compassion. Feel a sense of warmth and tenderness flowing through you, like the gentle caress of a warm summer breeze.

Take a few moments to bask in the nurturing energy of the Chicory flowers, knowing that you are always deserving of love and acceptance, both from yourself and from others.

When you feel ready, slowly bring your awareness back to the present moment. Wiggle your fingers and toes, gently stretch your body, and take a few more deep breaths.

Know that you can return to this inner sanctuary of self-love and acceptance whenever you need to reconnect with your own inherent worthiness.

When you're ready, you can slowly open your eyes and return to the world around you, carrying the sense of love and compassion with you.

9. Guided Meditation: Manifesting Presence with Bach Flower Clematis

Clematis

Find a quiet and comfortable space where you can sit or lie down without any distractions. Close your eyes gently, and take a few deep breaths, allowing yourself to settle into a state of relaxation.

As you continue to breathe deeply, bring your awareness to the center of your chest, the area of your heart. Visualize a soft, warm light glowing in this space, representing the energy of presence and awareness. Feel this light expanding with each breath, filling your entire being with a sense of groundedness and clarity.

Now, imagine yourself standing on the edge of a tranquil pond, surrounded by tall grasses and the gentle rustle of leaves in the breeze. Feel the earth beneath your feet, grounding you and connecting you to the natural world.

In the distance, you notice a cluster of Clematis flowers blooming with delicate petals. These flowers symbolize the Bach Flower Clematis remedy, which offers support for manifesting presence and staying grounded in the present moment.

With each step you take towards the Clematis flowers, feel yourself letting go of any distractions or worries that may be pulling you away from the here and now. Allow yourself to release the grip of daydreams and fantasies, and instead embrace a sense of rootedness and awareness.

As you reach the Clematis flowers, take a moment to observe their beauty and grace. Notice how they sway gently in the breeze, symbolizing the fluidity and presence that comes from being fully engaged in the present moment.

Now, imagine yourself sitting amidst the Clematis flowers, feeling their supportive energy surrounding you. Allow yourself to let go of any thoughts of the past or future, and instead focus on the sensations of the present moment.

With each breath, breathe in the essence of Clematis, allowing its healing energy to ground you in the here and now. Feel a sense of clarity and presence washing over you, like the gentle ripples on the surface of the pond.

Take a few moments to bask in the nurturing energy of the Clematis flowers, knowing that you are always supported and guided towards presence and awareness.

When you feel ready, slowly bring your awareness back to the present moment. Wiggle your fingers and toes, gently stretch your body, and take a few more deep breaths.

Know that you can return to this inner sanctuary of presence and awareness whenever you need to reconnect with the here and now.

When you're ready, you can slowly open your eyes and return to the world around you, carrying the sense of groundedness and clarity with you.

10. Guided Meditation: Embracing Self-Acceptance with Bach Flower Crab Apple

Crab Apple

Find a quiet and comfortable space where you can sit or lie down without any distractions. Close your eyes gently, and take a few deep breaths, allowing yourself to settle into a state of relaxation.

As you continue to breathe deeply, bring your awareness to the center of your chest, the area of your heart. Visualize a soft, warm light glowing in this space, representing the energy of self-acceptance and renewal. Feel this light expanding with each breath, filling your entire being with a sense of compassion and forgiveness.

Now, imagine yourself standing in a lush orchard, surrounded by trees heavy with ripe fruit. Feel the earth beneath your feet, grounding you and connecting you to the abundance of nature.

In the distance, you notice a Crab Apple tree standing tall and proud. Its branches are laden with tart, green apples, symbolizing the Bach Flower Crab Apple remedy, which offers support for embracing self-acceptance and releasing feelings of self-doubt and criticism.

With each step you take towards the Crab Apple tree, feel yourself letting go of any judgments or insecurities that may be weighing you down. Allow yourself to release the need for perfection and instead embrace a sense of wholeness and acceptance.

As you reach the Crab Apple tree, take a moment to observe its beauty and resilience. Notice how its branches stretch towards the sky, offering shelter and nourishment to all who seek it.

Now, imagine yourself sitting beneath the branches of the Crab Apple tree, feeling its supportive energy enveloping you. Allow yourself to open your heart to the love and acceptance that resides within you, knowing that you are worthy of compassion and forgiveness.

With each breath, breathe in the essence of Crab Apple, allowing its healing energy to wash over you and cleanse you of any lingering self-doubt or criticism. Feel a sense of renewal and liberation coursing through you, like the sweet juice of a ripe apple.

Take a few moments to bask in the nurturing energy of the Crab Apple tree, knowing that you are always supported and loved, just as you are.

When you feel ready, slowly bring your awareness back to the present moment. Wiggle your fingers and toes, gently stretch your body, and take a few more deep breaths.

Know that you can return to this inner sanctuary of self-acceptance and renewal whenever you need to reconnect with your own inherent worthiness.

When you're ready, you can slowly open your eyes and return to the world around you, carrying the sense of compassion and forgiveness with you.

11. Guided Meditation: Releasing Burdens with Bach Flower Elm

Elm

Find a quiet and comfortable space where you can sit or lie down without any distractions. Close your eyes gently, and take a few deep breaths, allowing yourself to settle into a state of relaxation.

As you continue to breathe deeply, bring your awareness to the center of your chest, the area of your heart. Visualize a soft, warm light glowing in this space, representing the energy of peace and tranquility. Feel this light expanding with each breath, filling your entire being with a sense of calmness and ease.

Now, imagine yourself standing at the edge of a serene lake, surrounded by towering trees and the soothing sounds of nature. Feel the earth beneath your feet, grounding you and connecting you to the natural world.

In the distance, you notice a majestic Elm tree standing tall and proud. Its branches reach towards the sky, offering shade and shelter to all who seek it. This tree symbolizes the Bach Flower Elm remedy, which offers support for releasing feelings of overwhelm and burden.

With each step you take towards the Elm tree, feel yourself letting go of any responsibilities or expectations that may be weighing you down. Allow yourself to release the need to carry the weight of the world on your shoulders, and instead embrace a sense of lightness and freedom.

As you reach the Elm tree, take a moment to observe its strength and resilience. Notice how its roots run deep into the earth, anchoring it firmly in place despite any storms that may come its way.

Now, imagine yourself sitting beneath the branches of the Elm tree, feeling its supportive energy enveloping you. Allow yourself to surrender to the peace and serenity of this sacred space, knowing that you are safe and protected here.

With each breath, breathe in the essence of Elm, allowing its healing energy to wash over you and lift any burdens from your heart and mind. Feel a sense of relief and release as you let go of anything that no longer serves you.

Take a few moments to bask in the nurturing energy of the Elm tree, knowing that you are always supported and guided towards peace and tranquility.

When you feel ready, slowly bring your awareness back to the present moment. Wiggle your fingers and toes, gently stretch your body, and take a few more deep breaths.

Know that you can return to this inner sanctuary of peace and ease whenever you need to reconnect with your own inner strength and resilience.

When you're ready, you can slowly open your eyes and return to the world around you, carrying the sense of lightness and freedom with you.

12. Guided Meditation: Cultivating Resilience with Bach Flower Gentian

Gentian

Find a quiet and comfortable space where you can sit or lie down without any distractions. Close your eyes gently, and take a few deep breaths, allowing yourself to settle into a state of relaxation.

As you continue to breathe deeply, bring your awareness to the center of your chest, the area of your heart. Visualize a soft, warm light glowing in this space, representing the energy of resilience and strength. Feel this light expanding with each breath, filling your entire being with a sense of courage and determination.

Now, imagine yourself standing on the edge of a lush meadow, surrounded by colorful wildflowers swaying gently in the breeze. Feel the earth beneath your feet, grounding you and connecting you to the natural world.

In the distance, you notice a cluster of Gentian flowers blooming with vibrant blue petals. These flowers symbolize the Bach Flower Gentian remedy, which offers support for overcoming setbacks and finding inner resilience.

With each step you take towards the Gentian flowers, feel yourself letting go of any doubts or disappointments that may be holding you back. Allow yourself to release the grip of negativity and instead embrace a sense of hope and optimism.

As you reach the Gentian flowers, take a moment to observe their beauty and grace. Notice how they stand tall and proud, symbolizing the strength and resilience that comes from facing challenges with courage and determination.

Now, imagine yourself sitting amidst the Gentian flowers, feeling their supportive energy surrounding you. Allow yourself to open your heart to the possibilities that lie ahead, knowing that every setback is an opportunity for growth and transformation.

With each breath, breathe in the essence of Gentian, allowing its healing energy to infuse you with a renewed sense of purpose and resolve. Feel a sense of determination and perseverance rising within you, like the steady march of a mountain stream.

Take a few moments to bask in the nurturing energy of the Gentian flowers, knowing that you are always supported and guided towards resilience and strength.

When you feel ready, slowly bring your awareness back to the present moment. Wiggle your fingers and toes, gently stretch your body, and take a few more deep breaths.

Know that you can return to this inner sanctuary of resilience and determination whenever you need to reconnect with your own inner strength.

When you're ready, you can slowly open your eyes and return to the world around you, carrying the sense of courage and optimism with you.

13. Guided Meditation: Embracing Hope and Renewal with Bach Flower Gorse

Gorse

Find a quiet and comfortable space where you can sit or lie down without any distractions. Close your eyes gently, and take a few deep breaths, allowing yourself to settle into a state of relaxation.

As you continue to breathe deeply, bring your awareness to the center of your chest, the area of your heart. Visualize a soft, warm light glowing in this space, representing the energy of hope and renewal. Feel this light expanding with each breath, filling your entire being with a sense of optimism and possibility.

Now, imagine yourself standing on the edge of a vast field, surrounded by rolling hills and the soft rustle of grass in the wind. Feel the earth beneath your feet, grounding you and connecting you to the natural world.

In the distance, you notice a cluster of Gorse bushes blooming with vibrant yellow flowers. These flowers symbolize the Bach Flower Gorse remedy, which offers support for finding hope and renewal in times of despair.

With each step you take towards the Gorse bushes, feel yourself letting go of any feelings of hopelessness or defeat that may be weighing you down. Allow yourself to release the grip of negativity and instead embrace a sense of faith and possibility.

As you reach the Gorse bushes, take a moment to observe their beauty and resilience. Notice how they stand tall and proud, symbolizing the strength and vitality that comes from embracing hope in the face of adversity.

Now, imagine yourself sitting amidst the Gorse bushes, feeling their supportive energy surrounding you. Allow yourself to open your heart to the light and warmth of hope, knowing that even in the darkest of times, there is always a glimmer of possibility.

With each breath, breathe in the essence of Gorse, allowing its healing energy to infuse you with a renewed sense of faith and optimism. Feel a sense of lightness and joy rising within you, like the first rays of sunlight breaking through the clouds after a storm.

Take a few moments to bask in the nurturing energy of the Gorse bushes, knowing that you are always supported and guided towards hope and renewal.

When you feel ready, slowly bring your awareness back to the present moment. Wiggle your fingers and toes, gently stretch your body, and take a few more deep breaths.

Know that you can return to this inner sanctuary of hope and possibility whenever you need to reconnect with your own inner light.

When you're ready, you can slowly open your eyes and return to the world around you, carrying the sense of optimism and renewal with you.

14. Guided Meditation: Cultivating Inner Peace with Bach Flower Heather

Heather

Find a quiet and comfortable space where you can sit or lie down without any distractions. Close your eyes gently, and take a few deep breaths, allowing yourself to settle into a state of relaxation.

As you continue to breathe deeply, bring your awareness to the center of your chest, the area of your heart. Visualize a soft, warm light glowing in this space, representing the energy of peace and tranquility. Feel this light expanding with each breath, filling your entire being with a sense of calmness and serenity.

Now, imagine yourself standing on a gentle hilltop, surrounded by rolling fields of vibrant heather in full bloom. Feel the earth beneath your feet, grounding you and connecting you to the beauty of the natural world.

In the distance, you notice a gentle breeze carrying the sweet scent of the heather flowers. These flowers symbolize the Bach Flower Heather remedy, which offers support for finding inner peace and connection.

With each step you take through the fields of heather, feel yourself letting go of any feelings of restlessness or anxiety that may be weighing you down. Allow yourself to release the grip of worry and instead embrace a sense of stillness and contentment.

As you immerse yourself in the beauty of the heather fields, take a moment to listen to the soothing sounds of nature all around you. Feel the gentle rhythm of your breath, syncing with the ebb and flow of life.

Now, imagine yourself sitting amidst the heather flowers, feeling their supportive energy enveloping you. Allow yourself to open your heart to the peace and tranquility that resides within you, knowing that you are always connected to the inherent wisdom of the universe.

With each breath, breathe in the essence of heather, allowing its healing energy to wash over you and soothe any inner turmoil or tension. Feel a sense of calmness and serenity spreading throughout your entire being, like the gentle caress of a summer breeze.

Take a few moments to bask in the nurturing energy of the heather fields, knowing that you are always supported and guided towards inner peace and harmony.

When you feel ready, slowly bring your awareness back to the present moment. Wiggle your fingers and toes, gently stretch your body, and take a few more deep breaths.

Know that you can return to this inner sanctuary of peace and tranquility whenever you need to reconnect with your own inner wisdom and serenity.

When you're ready, you can slowly open your eyes and return to the world around you, carrying the sense of calmness and contentment with you.

15. Guided Meditation: Cultivating Compassion and Harmony with Bach Flower Holly

Holly

Find a quiet and comfortable space where you can sit or lie down without any distractions. Close your eyes gently, and take a few deep breaths, allowing yourself to settle into a state of relaxation.

As you continue to breathe deeply, bring your awareness to the center of your chest, the area of your heart. Visualize a soft, warm light glowing in this space, representing the energy of compassion and harmony. Feel this light expanding with each breath, filling your entire being with a sense of openness and connection.

Now, imagine yourself standing in a peaceful forest, surrounded by tall trees and the gentle sounds of nature. Feel the earth beneath your feet, grounding you and connecting you to the natural world.

In the distance, you notice a Holly tree standing tall and proud. Its branches are adorned with bright red berries, symbolizing the Bach Flower Holly remedy, which offers support for cultivating compassion and harmony within oneself.

With each step you take towards the Holly tree, feel yourself letting go of any feelings of anger or resentment that may be weighing you down. Allow yourself to release the grip of negativity and instead embrace a sense of love and acceptance.

As you reach the Holly tree, take a moment to observe its beauty and resilience. Notice how its branches reach towards the sky, offering shelter and nourishment to all who seek it.

Now, imagine yourself sitting beneath the branches of the Holly tree, feeling its supportive energy enveloping you. Allow yourself to open your heart to the love and compassion that resides within you, knowing that you are worthy of kindness and understanding.

With each breath, breathe in the essence of Holly, allowing its healing energy to wash over you and soften any feelings of anger or resentment. Feel a sense of peace and harmony spreading throughout your entire being, like the gentle rustle of leaves in the wind.

Take a few moments to bask in the nurturing energy of the Holly tree, knowing that you are always supported and guided towards compassion and harmony.

When you feel ready, slowly bring your awareness back to the present moment. Wiggle your fingers and toes, gently stretch your body, and take a few more deep breaths.

Know that you can return to this inner sanctuary of love and acceptance whenever you need to reconnect with your own inherent worthiness.

When you're ready, you can slowly open your eyes and return to the world around you, carrying the sense of compassion and harmony with you.

16. Guided Meditation: Embracing the Present with Bach Flower Honeysuckle

Honeysuckle

Find a quiet and comfortable space where you can sit or lie down without any distractions. Close your eyes gently, and take a few deep breaths, allowing yourself to settle into a state of relaxation.

As you continue to breathe deeply, bring your awareness to the center of your chest, the area of your heart. Visualize a soft, warm light glowing in this space, representing the energy of the present moment. Feel this light expanding with each breath, filling your entire being with a sense of presence and awareness.

Now, imagine yourself standing in a beautiful garden, surrounded by lush greenery and the delicate scent of flowers in bloom. Feel the earth beneath your feet, grounding you and connecting you to the abundance of nature.

In the distance, you notice a Honeysuckle vine winding its way around a trellis, its fragrant blossoms in full bloom. This vine symbolizes the Bach Flower Honeysuckle remedy, which offers support for embracing the present and letting go of the past.

With each step you take towards the Honeysuckle vine, feel yourself letting go of any feelings of nostalgia or longing that may be pulling you away from the present moment. Allow yourself to release the grip of memories and instead embrace a sense of presence and gratitude for the here and now.

As you reach the Honeysuckle vine, take a moment to observe its beauty and grace. Notice how its tendrils reach out towards the sun, symbolizing the unfolding of new experiences and opportunities in the present moment.

Now, imagine yourself sitting beside the Honeysuckle vine, feeling its supportive energy surrounding you. Allow yourself to open your heart to the richness and beauty of the present moment, knowing that life is always unfolding in new and unexpected ways.

With each breath, breathe in the essence of Honeysuckle, allowing its healing energy to wash over you and anchor you in the here and now. Feel a sense of peace and contentment spreading throughout your entire being, like the gentle caress of a summer breeze.

Take a few moments to bask in the nurturing energy of the Honeysuckle vine, knowing that you are always supported and guided towards presence and awareness.

When you feel ready, slowly bring your awareness back to the present moment. Wiggle your fingers and toes, gently stretch your body, and take a few more deep breaths.

Know that you can return to this inner sanctuary of presence and gratitude whenever you need to reconnect with the richness of the present moment.

When you're ready, you can slowly open your eyes and return to the world around you, carrying the sense of presence and gratitude with you.

17. Guided Meditation: Renewing Energy with Bach Flower Hornbeam

Hornbeam

Find a quiet and comfortable space where you can sit or lie down without any distractions. Close your eyes gently, and take a few deep breaths, allowing yourself to settle into a state of relaxation.

As you continue to breathe deeply, bring your awareness to the center of your chest, the area of your heart. Visualize a soft, warm light glowing in this space, representing the energy of vitality and renewal. Feel this light expanding with each breath, filling your entire being with a sense of rejuvenation and strength.

Now, imagine yourself standing in a peaceful forest, surrounded by tall trees and the gentle sounds of nature. Feel the earth beneath your feet, grounding you and connecting you to the abundance of life all around you.

In the distance, you notice a majestic Hornbeam tree standing tall and proud. Its branches are adorned with fresh green leaves, symbolizing the Bach Flower Hornbeam remedy, which offers support for renewing energy and overcoming feelings of fatigue or lethargy.

With each step you take towards the Hornbeam tree, feel yourself letting go of any feelings of weariness or doubt that may be weighing you down. Allow yourself to release the grip of exhaustion and instead embrace a sense of vitality and enthusiasm for life.

As you reach the Hornbeam tree, take a moment to observe its beauty and resilience. Notice how its branches reach towards the sky, symbolizing the upward movement of energy and growth.

Now, imagine yourself sitting beneath the branches of the Hornbeam tree, feeling its supportive energy enveloping you. Allow yourself to open your heart to the renewal of energy and vitality that resides within you, knowing that you are capable of overcoming any challenges that come your way.

With each breath, breathe in the essence of Hornbeam, allowing its healing energy to wash over you and invigorate your spirit. Feel a sense of clarity and purpose rising within you, like the first rays of sunlight breaking through the canopy of trees.

Take a few moments to bask in the nurturing energy of the Hornbeam tree, knowing that you are always supported and guided towards renewed energy and strength.

When you feel ready, slowly bring your awareness back to the present moment. Wiggle your fingers and toes, gently stretch your body, and take a few more deep breaths.

Know that you can return to this inner sanctuary of renewal and vitality whenever you need to reconnect with your own inner strength.

When you're ready, you can slowly open your eyes and return to the world around you, carrying the sense of energy and vitality with you.

18. Guided Meditation: Embracing Patience and Serenity with Bach Flower Impatiens

Impatiens

Find a quiet and comfortable space where you can sit or lie down without any distractions. Close your eyes gently, and take a few deep breaths, allowing yourself to settle into a state of relaxation.

As you continue to breathe deeply, bring your awareness to the center of your chest, the area of your heart. Visualize a soft, warm light glowing in this space, representing the energy of patience and serenity. Feel this light expanding with each breath, filling your entire being with a sense of calmness and tranquility.

Now, imagine yourself standing beside a gentle stream, surrounded by lush greenery and the soothing sounds of flowing water. Feel the earth beneath your feet, grounding you and connecting you to the natural world.

In the distance, you notice a cluster of Impatiens flowers blooming with vibrant colors. These flowers symbolize the Bach Flower Impatiens remedy, which offers support for cultivating patience and inner peace.

With each step you take towards the Impatiens flowers, feel yourself letting go of any feelings of impatience or frustration that may be weighing you down. Allow yourself to release the grip of tension and instead embrace a sense of ease and acceptance.

As you reach the Impatiens flowers, take a moment to observe their delicate beauty and grace. Notice how they sway gently in the breeze, symbolizing the fluidity and grace that comes from being in harmony with the present moment.

Now, imagine yourself sitting amidst the Impatiens flowers, feeling their supportive energy surrounding you. Allow yourself to open your heart to the peace and tranquility that resides within you, knowing that you are always supported and guided towards patience and serenity.

With each breath, breathe in the essence of Impatiens, allowing its healing energy to wash over you and soothe any inner turmoil or agitation. Feel a sense of calmness and tranquility spreading throughout your entire being, like the gentle ripple of water on the surface of the stream.

Take a few moments to bask in the nurturing energy of the Impatiens flowers, knowing that you are always supported and guided towards patience and serenity.

When you feel ready, slowly bring your awareness back to the present moment. Wiggle your fingers and toes, gently stretch your body, and take a few more deep breaths.

Know that you can return to this inner sanctuary of peace and tranquility whenever you need to reconnect with your own inner wisdom and serenity.

When you're ready, you can slowly open your eyes and return to the world around you, carrying the sense of patience and serenity with you.

19. Guided Meditation: Cultivating Confidence and Self-Belief with Bach Flower Larch

Larch

Find a quiet and comfortable space where you can sit or lie down without any distractions. Close your eyes gently, and take a few deep breaths, allowing yourself to settle into a state of relaxation.

As you continue to breathe deeply, bring your awareness to the center of your chest, the area of your heart. Visualize a soft, warm light glowing in this space, representing the energy of confidence and self-belief. Feel this light expanding with each breath, filling your entire being with a sense of empowerment and assurance.

Now, imagine yourself standing at the edge of a lush forest, surrounded by tall trees and the gentle rustle of leaves in the breeze. Feel the earth beneath your feet, grounding you and connecting you to the strength of the natural world.

In the distance, you notice a majestic Larch tree standing tall and proud. Its branches are adorned with vibrant green needles, symbolizing the Bach Flower Larch remedy, which offers support for cultivating confidence and overcoming feelings of self-doubt.

With each step you take towards the Larch tree, feel yourself letting go of any limiting beliefs or negative self-talk that may be holding you back. Allow yourself to release the grip of fear and insecurity and instead embrace a sense of inner strength and resilience.

As you reach the Larch tree, take a moment to observe its beauty and majesty. Notice how it stands tall and unyielding, symbolizing the unwavering confidence that comes from believing in yourself.

Now, imagine yourself sitting beneath the branches of the Larch tree, feeling its supportive energy enveloping you. Allow yourself to open your heart to the limitless potential that resides within you, knowing that you are capable of achieving anything you set your mind to.

With each breath, breathe in the essence of Larch, allowing its healing energy to infuse you with a renewed sense of confidence and self-assurance. Feel a sense of empowerment and determination rising within you, like the steady growth of the tree's branches reaching towards the sky.

Take a few moments to bask in the nurturing energy of the Larch tree, knowing that you are always supported and guided towards success and fulfillment.

When you feel ready, slowly bring your awareness back to the present moment. Wiggle your fingers and toes, gently stretch your body, and take a few more deep breaths.

Know that you can return to this inner sanctuary of confidence and self-belief whenever you need to reconnect with your own inner strength.

When you're ready, you can slowly open your eyes and return to the world around you, carrying the sense of empowerment and assurance with you.

20. Guided Meditation: Embracing Courage and Inner Strength with Bach Flower Mimulus

Mimulus

Find a quiet and comfortable space where you can sit or lie down without any distractions. Close your eyes gently, and take a few deep breaths, allowing yourself to settle into a state of relaxation.

As you continue to breathe deeply, bring your awareness to the center of your chest, the area of your heart. Visualize a soft, warm light glowing in this space, representing the energy of courage and inner strength. Feel this light expanding with each breath, filling your entire being with a sense of bravery and empowerment.

Now, imagine yourself standing on the bank of a calm river, surrounded by lush greenery and the peaceful sounds of nature. Feel the earth beneath your feet, grounding you and connecting you to the stability of the natural world.

In the distance, you notice a cluster of Mimulus flowers blooming with vibrant hues. These flowers symbolize the Bach Flower Mimulus remedy, which offers support for overcoming fears and finding inner courage.

With each step you take towards the Mimulus flowers, feel yourself letting go of any worries or anxieties that may be holding you back. Allow yourself to release the grip of fear and instead embrace a sense of bravery and resilience.

As you reach the Mimulus flowers, take a moment to observe their beauty and grace. Notice how they stand tall and proud, symbolizing the strength and courage that comes from facing your fears head-on.

Now, imagine yourself sitting amidst the Mimulus flowers, feeling their supportive energy enveloping you. Allow yourself to open your heart to the courage and inner strength that resides within you, knowing that you are capable of overcoming any obstacles that come your way.

With each breath, breathe in the essence of Mimulus, allowing its healing energy to wash over you and fortify your spirit. Feel a sense of empowerment and determination rising within you, like the steady flow of the river beside you.

Take a few moments to bask in the nurturing energy of the Mimulus flowers, knowing that you are always supported and guided towards courage and resilience.

When you feel ready, slowly bring your awareness back to the present moment. Wiggle your fingers and toes, gently stretch your body, and take a few more deep breaths.

Know that you can return to this inner sanctuary of bravery and empowerment whenever you need to reconnect with your own inner strength.

When you're ready, you can slowly open your eyes and return to the world around you, carrying the sense of courage and inner strength with you.

21. Guided Meditation: Finding Light in Darkness with Bach Flower Mustard

Mustard

Find a quiet and comfortable space where you can sit or lie down without any distractions. Close your eyes gently, and take a few deep breaths, allowing yourself to settle into a state of relaxation.

As you continue to breathe deeply, bring your awareness to the center of your chest, the area of your heart. Visualize a soft, warm light glowing in this space, representing the energy of hope and illumination. Feel this light expanding with each breath, filling your entire being with a sense of warmth and reassurance.

Now, imagine yourself standing in a vast field, surrounded by tall grass and the gentle sway of wildflowers. Feel the earth beneath your feet, grounding you and connecting you to the beauty of the natural world.

In the distance, you notice a thick fog rolling in, casting a shadow over the landscape. This fog symbolizes the darkness and despair that can sometimes cloud our minds, as represented by the Bach Flower Mustard remedy.

With each step you take into the fog, feel yourself letting go of any feelings of sadness or heaviness that may be weighing you down. Allow yourself to release the grip of darkness and instead embrace a sense of openness and receptivity to the light.

As you move deeper into the fog, take a moment to acknowledge any emotions that arise within you. Allow yourself to sit with these feelings without judgment, knowing that it's okay to experience moments of darkness in life.

Now, imagine a flicker of light appearing in the distance, cutting through the fog with its radiant glow. This light symbolizes the hope and healing that comes from within, even in the darkest of times.

With each step towards the light, feel a sense of warmth and comfort washing over you. Allow yourself to open your heart to the possibility of healing and renewal, knowing that there is always light at the end of the tunnel.

As you reach the source of the light, take a moment to bask in its brilliance. Feel its soothing energy enveloping you, filling you with a sense of peace and serenity.

With each breath, breathe in the essence of Mustard, allowing its healing energy to wash over you and lift any lingering feelings of darkness or despair. Feel a sense of lightness and clarity spreading throughout your entire being, like the sun breaking through the clouds after a storm.

Take a few moments to bask in the nurturing energy of the light, knowing that you are always supported and guided towards hope and illumination.

When you feel ready, slowly bring your awareness back to the present moment. Wiggle your fingers and toes, gently stretch your body, and take a few more deep breaths.

Know that you can return to this inner sanctuary of light and healing whenever you need to reconnect with your own inner strength.

When you're ready, you can slowly open your eyes and return to the world around you, carrying the sense of hope and illumination with you.

22. Guided Meditation: Embracing Resilience and Surrender with Bach Flower Oak

Oak

Find a quiet and comfortable space where you can sit or lie down without any distractions. Close your eyes gently, and take a few deep breaths, allowing yourself to settle into a state of relaxation.

As you continue to breathe deeply, bring your awareness to the center of your chest, the area of your heart. Visualize a soft, warm light glowing in this space, representing the energy of resilience and surrender. Feel this light expanding with each breath, filling your entire being with a sense of strength and acceptance.

Now, imagine yourself standing in a vast forest, surrounded by towering oak trees and the gentle rustle of leaves in the breeze. Feel the earth beneath your feet, grounding you and connecting you to the stability of the natural world.

In the distance, you notice a mighty Oak tree standing tall and proud. Its branches reach towards the sky, offering shelter and support to all who seek it. This tree symbolizes the Bach Flower Oak remedy, which offers support for embracing resilience and surrendering to the flow of life.

With each step you take towards the Oak tree, feel yourself letting go of any feelings of stubbornness or resistance that may be weighing you down. Allow yourself to release the grip of control and instead embrace a sense of surrender and trust in the universe.

As you reach the Oak tree, take a moment to observe its beauty and strength. Notice how its roots run deep into the earth, anchoring it firmly in place despite any storms that may come its way.

Now, imagine yourself sitting beneath the branches of the Oak tree, feeling its supportive energy enveloping you. Allow yourself to open your heart to the wisdom and resilience that resides within you, knowing that you are capable of weathering any challenges that come your way.

With each breath, breathe in the essence of Oak, allowing its healing energy to wash over you and infuse you with a renewed sense of strength and determination. Feel a sense of peace and serenity spreading throughout your entire being, like the gentle rustle of leaves in the wind.

Take a few moments to bask in the nurturing energy of the Oak tree, knowing that you are always supported and guided towards resilience and surrender.

When you feel ready, slowly bring your awareness back to the present moment. Wiggle your fingers and toes, gently stretch your body, and take a few more deep breaths.

Know that you can return to this inner sanctuary of strength and acceptance whenever you need to reconnect with your own inner wisdom.

When you're ready, you can slowly open your eyes and return to the world around you, carrying the sense of resilience and surrender with you.

23. Guided Meditation: Restoring Energy and Vitality with Bach Flower Olive

Olive

Find a quiet and comfortable space where you can sit or lie down without any distractions. Close your eyes gently, and take a few deep breaths, allowing yourself to settle into a state of relaxation.

As you continue to breathe deeply, bring your awareness to the center of your chest, the area of your heart. Visualize a soft, warm light glowing in this space, representing the energy of renewal and vitality. Feel this light expanding with each breath, filling your entire being with a sense of rejuvenation and strength.

Now, imagine yourself standing in a serene olive grove, surrounded by rows of ancient trees and the gentle rustle of leaves in the breeze. Feel the earth beneath your feet, grounding you and connecting you to the timeless energy of the natural world.

In the distance, you notice a majestic Olive tree standing tall and proud. Its branches are laden with ripe fruit, symbolizing the Bach Flower Olive remedy, which offers support for restoring energy and vitality after periods of exhaustion.

With each step you take towards the Olive tree, feel yourself letting go of any feelings of fatigue or depletion that may be weighing you down. Allow yourself to release the grip of weariness and instead embrace a sense of renewal and vitality.

As you reach the Olive tree, take a moment to observe its beauty and resilience. Notice how its branches stretch towards the sky, reaching for the warmth of the sun and the nourishment of the earth.

Now, imagine yourself sitting beneath the branches of the Olive tree, feeling its supportive energy enveloping you. Allow yourself to open your heart to the healing and rejuvenating energy that surrounds you, knowing that you are always supported and guided towards restoration and renewal.

With each breath, breathe in the essence of Olive, allowing its healing energy to wash over you and revitalize your spirit. Feel a sense of warmth and vitality spreading throughout your entire being, like the gentle glow of sunlight filtering through the leaves.

Take a few moments to bask in the nurturing energy of the Olive tree, knowing that you are always supported and guided towards health and well-being.

When you feel ready, slowly bring your awareness back to the present moment. Wiggle your fingers and toes, gently stretch your body, and take a few more deep breaths.

Know that you can return to this inner sanctuary of renewal and vitality whenever you need to reconnect with your own inner strength.

When you're ready, you can slowly open your eyes and return to the world around you, carrying the sense of energy and vitality with you.

24. Guided Meditation: Releasing Guilt and Embracing Self-Acceptance with Bach Flower Pine

Pine

Find a quiet and comfortable space where you can sit or lie down without any distractions. Close your eyes gently, and take a few deep breaths, allowing yourself to settle into a state of relaxation.

As you continue to breathe deeply, bring your awareness to the center of your chest, the area of your heart. Visualize a soft, warm light glowing in this space, representing the energy of self-acceptance and forgiveness. Feel this light expanding with each breath, filling your entire being with a sense of compassion and understanding.

Now, imagine yourself standing in a serene pine forest, surrounded by tall trees and the earthy scent of pine needles. Feel the earth beneath your feet, grounding you and connecting you to the healing energy of nature.

In the distance, you notice a majestic Pine tree standing tall and proud. Its branches are laden with lush green needles, symbolizing the Bach Flower Pine remedy, which offers support for releasing guilt and embracing self-acceptance.

With each step you take towards the Pine tree, feel yourself letting go of any feelings of inadequacy or self-blame that may be weighing you down. Allow yourself to release the grip of guilt and instead embrace a sense of self-love and acceptance.

As you reach the Pine tree, take a moment to observe its beauty and resilience. Notice how it stands tall and strong, symbolizing the strength and resilience that comes from accepting yourself exactly as you are.

Now, imagine yourself sitting beneath the branches of the Pine tree, feeling its supportive energy enveloping you. Allow yourself to open your heart to the healing and forgiveness that resides within you, knowing that you are worthy of love and acceptance just as you are.

With each breath, breathe in the essence of Pine, allowing its healing energy to wash over you and release any lingering feelings of guilt or shame. Feel a sense of lightness and freedom spreading throughout your entire being, like the gentle rustle of pine needles in the wind.

Take a few moments to bask in the nurturing energy of the Pine tree, knowing that you are always supported and guided towards self-acceptance and forgiveness.

When you feel ready, slowly bring your awareness back to the present moment. Wiggle your fingers and toes, gently stretch your body, and take a few more deep breaths.

Know that you can return to this inner sanctuary of self-acceptance and forgiveness whenever you need to reconnect with your own inherent worthiness.

When you're ready, you can slowly open your eyes and return to the world around you, carrying the sense of compassion and self-acceptance with you.

25. Guided Meditation: Cultivating Inner Peace and Trust with Bach Flower Red Chestnut

Red Chestnut

Find a quiet and comfortable space where you can sit or lie down without any distractions. Close your eyes gently, and take a few deep breaths, allowing yourself to settle into a state of relaxation.

As you continue to breathe deeply, bring your awareness to the center of your chest, the area of your heart. Visualize a soft, warm light glowing in this space, representing the energy of peace and trust. Feel this light expanding with each breath, filling your entire being with a sense of calmness and assurance.

Now, imagine yourself standing beside a tranquil river, surrounded by lush greenery and the gentle sounds of nature. Feel the earth beneath your feet, grounding you and connecting you to the abundance of life all around you.

In the distance, you notice a majestic Chestnut tree standing tall and proud. Its branches are adorned with vibrant red chestnuts, symbolizing the Bach Flower Red Chestnut remedy, which offers support for releasing worries and cultivating trust in the flow of life.

With each step you take towards the Chestnut tree, feel yourself letting go of any feelings of anxiety or fear that may be weighing you down. Allow yourself to release the grip of worry and instead embrace a sense of peace and trust in the universe.

As you reach the Chestnut tree, take a moment to observe its beauty and strength. Notice how its roots run deep into the earth, anchoring it firmly in place despite any storms that may come its way.

Now, imagine yourself sitting beneath the branches of the Chestnut tree, feeling its supportive energy enveloping you. Allow yourself to open your heart to the peace and trust that resides within you, knowing that you are always supported and guided towards safety and security.

With each breath, breathe in the essence of Red Chestnut, allowing its healing energy to wash over you and soothe any worries or anxieties. Feel a sense of calmness and assurance spreading throughout your entire being, like the gentle flow of the river beside you.

Take a few moments to bask in the nurturing energy of the Chestnut tree, knowing that you are always supported and guided towards inner peace and trust.

When you feel ready, slowly bring your awareness back to the present moment. Wiggle your fingers and toes, gently stretch your body, and take a few more deep breaths.

Know that you can return to this inner sanctuary of peace and trust whenever you need to reconnect with your own inner wisdom and security.

When you're ready, you can slowly open your eyes and return to the world around you, carrying the sense of peace and trust with you.

26. Guided Meditation: Finding Courage and Calmness with Bach Flower Rock Rose

Rock Rose

Find a quiet and comfortable space where you can sit or lie down without any distractions. Close your eyes gently, and take a few deep breaths, allowing yourself to settle into a state of relaxation.

As you continue to breathe deeply, bring your awareness to the center of your chest, the area of your heart. Visualize a soft, warm light glowing in this space, representing the energy of courage and calmness. Feel this light expanding with each breath, filling your entire being with a sense of strength and tranquility.

Now, imagine yourself standing on a peaceful mountaintop, surrounded by the beauty of nature and the vast expanse of the sky above. Feel the earth beneath your feet, grounding you and connecting you to the stability of the natural world.

In the distance, you notice a cluster of Rockrose flowers blooming with vibrant colors. These flowers symbolize the Bach Flower Rock Rose remedy, which offers support for finding courage in moments of fear and panic.

With each step you take towards the Rockrose flowers, feel yourself letting go of any feelings of anxiety or uncertainty that may be weighing you down. Allow yourself to release the grip of fear and instead embrace a sense of bravery and calmness.

As you reach the Rockrose flowers, take a moment to observe their beauty and resilience. Notice how they stand tall and proud, symbolizing the strength and courage that comes from facing your fears head-on.

Now, imagine yourself sitting amidst the Rockrose flowers, feeling their supportive energy enveloping you. Allow yourself to open your heart to the courage and calmness that resides within you, knowing that you are capable of overcoming any challenges that come your way.

With each breath, breathe in the essence of Rockrose, allowing its healing energy to wash over you and fill you with a sense of peace and tranquility. Feel a sense of empowerment and serenity spreading throughout your entire being, like the gentle rustle of leaves in the wind.

Take a few moments to bask in the nurturing energy of the Rockrose flowers, knowing that you are always supported and guided towards courage and calmness.

When you feel ready, slowly bring your awareness back to the present moment. Wiggle your fingers and toes, gently stretch your body, and take a few more deep breaths.

Know that you can return to this inner sanctuary of courage and calmness whenever you need to reconnect with your own inner strength.

When you're ready, you can slowly open your eyes and return to the world around you, carrying the sense of bravery and tranquility with you.

27. Guided Meditation: Finding Balance and Flexibility with Bach Flower Rock Water

Rock water

Find a quiet and comfortable space where you can sit or lie down without any distractions. Close your eyes gently, and take a few deep breaths, allowing yourself to settle into a state of relaxation.

As you continue to breathe deeply, bring your awareness to the center of your chest, the area of your heart. Visualize a soft, warm light glowing in this space, representing the energy of balance and flexibility. Feel this light expanding with each breath, filling your entire being with a sense of harmony and adaptability.

Now, imagine yourself standing at the edge of a serene lake, surrounded by towering cliffs and the gentle lapping of water against the shore. Feel the earth beneath your feet, grounding you and connecting you to the stability of the natural world.

In the distance, you notice a waterfall cascading down the cliffs, its waters flowing with grace and fluidity. This waterfall symbolizes the Bach Flower Rock Water remedy, which offers support for finding balance and embracing change.

With each step you take towards the waterfall, feel yourself letting go of any feelings of rigidity or stubbornness that may be holding you back. Allow yourself to release the grip of perfectionism and instead embrace a sense of openness and flexibility.

As you reach the base of the waterfall, take a moment to observe its beauty and power. Notice how the water flows effortlessly over the rocks, adapting to the contours of the land without resistance.

Now, imagine yourself sitting beside the waterfall, feeling its rejuvenating energy enveloping you. Allow yourself to open your heart to the balance and flexibility that resides within you, knowing that you are capable of navigating the ebb and flow of life with grace.

With each breath, breathe in the essence of Rock Water, allowing its healing energy to wash over you and fill you with a sense of harmony and adaptability. Feel a sense of peace and serenity spreading throughout your entire being, like the gentle flow of water over smooth rocks.

Take a few moments to bask in the nurturing energy of the waterfall, knowing that you are always supported and guided towards balance and flexibility.

When you feel ready, slowly bring your awareness back to the present moment. Wiggle your fingers and toes, gently stretch your body, and take a few more deep breaths.

Know that you can return to this inner sanctuary of balance and flexibility whenever you need to reconnect with your own inner wisdom.

When you're ready, you can slowly open your eyes and return to the world around you, carrying the sense of harmony and adaptability with you.

28. Guided Meditation: Finding Inner Balance and Certainty with Bach Flower Scleranthus

Scleranthus

Find a quiet and comfortable space where you can sit or lie down without any distractions. Close your eyes gently, and take a few deep breaths, allowing yourself to settle into a state of relaxation.

As you continue to breathe deeply, bring your awareness to the center of your chest, the area of your heart. Visualize a soft, warm light glowing in this space, representing the energy of inner balance and certainty. Feel this light expanding with each breath, filling your entire being with a sense of steadiness and assurance.

Now, imagine yourself standing in a beautiful garden, surrounded by colorful flowers and the gentle hum of bees. Feel the earth beneath your feet, grounding you and connecting you to the abundance of life all around you.

In the distance, you notice a cluster of Scleranthus flowers swaying gently in the breeze. These flowers symbolize the Bach Flower Scleranthus remedy, which offers support for finding balance and making decisions with confidence.

With each step you take towards the Scleranthus flowers, feel yourself letting go of any feelings of indecision or uncertainty that may be weighing you down. Allow yourself to release the grip of doubt and instead embrace a sense of clarity and certainty.

As you reach the Scleranthus flowers, take a moment to observe their beauty and simplicity. Notice how they stand tall and proud, symbolizing the strength and resolve that comes from finding inner balance.

Now, imagine yourself sitting amidst the Scleranthus flowers, feeling their supportive energy enveloping you. Allow yourself to open your heart to the balance and certainty that resides within you, knowing that you are capable of making choices with confidence and conviction.

With each breath, breathe in the essence of Scleranthus, allowing its healing energy to wash over you and fill you with a sense of inner peace and assurance. Feel a sense of alignment and harmony spreading throughout your entire being, like the delicate dance of the flowers in the wind.

Take a few moments to bask in the nurturing energy of the Scleranthus flowers, knowing that you are always supported and guided towards balance and certainty.

When you feel ready, slowly bring your awareness back to the present moment. Wiggle your fingers and toes, gently stretch your body, and take a few more deep breaths.

Know that you can return to this inner sanctuary of balance and certainty whenever you need to reconnect with your own inner wisdom.

When you're ready, you can slowly open your eyes and return to the world around you, carrying the sense of clarity and assurance with you.

29. Guided Meditation: Healing and Releasing with Bach Flower Star of Bethlehem

Star of Bethlehem

Find a quiet and comfortable space where you can sit or lie down without any distractions. Close your eyes gently, and take a few deep breaths, allowing yourself to settle into a state of relaxation.

As you continue to breathe deeply, bring your awareness to the center of your chest, the area of your heart. Visualize a soft, warm light glowing in this space, representing the energy of healing and release. Feel this light expanding with each breath, filling your entire being with a sense of comfort and peace.

Now, imagine yourself standing in a tranquil meadow, surrounded by wildflowers and the gentle rustle of grass in the breeze. Feel the earth beneath your feet, grounding you and connecting you to the nurturing energy of the natural world.

In the distance, you notice a radiant Star of Bethlehem flower blooming with ethereal beauty. This flower symbolizes the Bach Flower Star of Bethlehem remedy, which offers support for healing emotional wounds and finding solace in times of distress.

With each step you take towards the Star of Bethlehem flower, feel yourself letting go of any lingering pain or sorrow that may be weighing you down. Allow yourself to release the grip of past traumas and instead embrace a sense of peace and renewal.

As you reach the Star of Bethlehem flower, take a moment to observe its delicate petals and soothing fragrance. Notice how it radiates a gentle warmth and compassion, inviting you to let go of any burdens you may be carrying.

Now, imagine yourself sitting beside the Star of Bethlehem flower, feeling its healing energy enveloping you. Allow yourself to open your heart to the healing and release that resides within you, knowing that you are always supported and guided towards wholeness.

With each breath, breathe in the essence of Star of Bethlehem, allowing its healing energy to wash over you and soothe any emotional wounds. Feel a sense of comfort and serenity spreading throughout your entire being, like a warm embrace from the universe.

Take a few moments to bask in the nurturing energy of the Star of Bethlehem flower, knowing that you are always supported and guided towards healing and renewal.

When you feel ready, slowly bring your awareness back to the present moment. Wiggle your fingers and toes, gently stretch your body, and take a few more deep breaths.

Know that you can return to this inner sanctuary of healing and release whenever you need to reconnect with your own inner strength.

When you're ready, you can slowly open your eyes and return to the world around you, carrying the sense of comfort and peace with you.

30. Guided Meditation: Embracing Hope and Renewal with Bach Flower Sweet Chestnut

Sweet Chestnut

Find a quiet and comfortable space where you can sit or lie down without any distractions. Close your eyes gently, and take a few deep breaths, allowing yourself to settle into a state of relaxation.

As you continue to breathe deeply, bring your awareness to the center of your chest, the area of your heart. Visualize a soft, warm light glowing in this space, representing the energy of hope and renewal. Feel this light expanding with each breath, filling your entire being with a sense of comfort and resilience.

Now, imagine yourself standing in a serene forest, surrounded by tall trees and the gentle whisper of the wind in the leaves. Feel the earth beneath your feet, grounding you and connecting you to the healing energy of the natural world.

In the distance, you notice a majestic Sweet Chestnut tree standing tall and proud. Its branches are adorned with vibrant green leaves, symbolizing the Bach Flower Sweet Chestnut remedy, which offers support for finding hope and solace in times of despair.

With each step you take towards the Sweet Chestnut tree, feel yourself letting go of any feelings of darkness or despair that may be weighing you down. Allow yourself to release the grip of anguish and instead embrace a sense of lightness and renewal.

As you reach the Sweet Chestnut tree, take a moment to observe its beauty and strength. Notice how it stands tall and unwavering, symbolizing the resilience and endurance of the human spirit.

Now, imagine yourself sitting beneath the branches of the Sweet Chestnut tree, feeling its supportive energy enveloping you. Allow yourself to open your heart to the hope and renewal that resides within you, knowing that you are capable of finding light even in the darkest of times.

With each breath, breathe in the essence of Sweet Chestnut, allowing its healing energy to wash over you and fill you with a sense of comfort and reassurance. Feel a sense of peace and tranquility spreading throughout your entire being, like the gentle rustle of leaves in the wind.

Take a few moments to bask in the nurturing energy of the Sweet Chestnut tree, knowing that you are always supported and guided towards hope and renewal.

When you feel ready, slowly bring your awareness back to the present moment. Wiggle your fingers and toes, gently stretch your body, and take a few more deep breaths.

Know that you can return to this inner sanctuary of hope and renewal whenever you need to reconnect with your own inner strength.

When you're ready, you can slowly open your eyes and return to the world around you, carrying the sense of comfort and resilience with you.

31. Guided Meditation: Cultivating Balance and Relaxation with Bach Flower Vervain

Vervain

Find a quiet and comfortable space where you can sit or lie down without any distractions. Close your eyes gently, and take a few deep breaths, allowing yourself to settle into a state of relaxation.

As you continue to breathe deeply, bring your awareness to the center of your chest, the area of your heart. Visualize a soft, warm light glowing in this space, representing the energy of balance and relaxation. Feel this light expanding with each breath, filling your entire being with a sense of calmness and tranquility.

Now, imagine yourself standing in a lush meadow, surrounded by wildflowers and the gentle rustle of grass in the breeze. Feel the earth beneath your feet, grounding you and connecting you to the nurturing energy of the natural world.

In the distance, you notice a cluster of Vervain flowers swaying gently in the wind. These flowers symbolize the Bach Flower Vervain remedy, which offers support for finding balance and relaxation amidst busyness and intensity.

With each step you take towards the Vervain flowers, feel yourself letting go of any feelings of tension or overwhelm that may be weighing you down. Allow yourself to release the grip of stress and instead embrace a sense of ease and tranquility.

As you reach the Vervain flowers, take a moment to observe their beauty and grace. Notice how they sway gently in the breeze, symbolizing the fluidity and adaptability of the natural world.

Now, imagine yourself sitting amidst the Vervain flowers, feeling their supportive energy enveloping you. Allow yourself to open your heart to the balance and relaxation that resides within you, knowing that you are capable of finding peace in any situation.

With each breath, breathe in the essence of Vervain, allowing its healing energy to wash over you and fill you with a sense of calmness and serenity. Feel a sense of lightness and relaxation spreading throughout your entire being, like the gentle sway of the flowers in the wind.

Take a few moments to bask in the nurturing energy of the Vervain flowers, knowing that you are always supported and guided towards balance and relaxation.

When you feel ready, slowly bring your awareness back to the present moment. Wiggle your fingers and toes, gently stretch your body, and take a few more deep breaths.

Know that you can return to this inner sanctuary of balance and relaxation whenever you need to reconnect with your own inner peace.

When you're ready, you can slowly open your eyes and return to the world around you, carrying the sense of calmness and tranquility with you.

32. Guided Meditation: Cultivating Compassion and Flexibility with Bach Flower Vine

Vine

Find a quiet and comfortable space where you can sit or lie down without any distractions. Close your eyes gently, and take a few deep breaths, allowing yourself to settle into a state of relaxation.

As you continue to breathe deeply, bring your awareness to the center of your chest, the area of your heart. Visualize a soft, warm light glowing in this space, representing the energy of compassion and flexibility. Feel this light expanding with each breath, filling your entire being with a sense of openness and kindness.

Now, imagine yourself standing in a lush vineyard, surrounded by rows of grapevines and the gentle rustle of leaves in the breeze. Feel the earth beneath your feet, grounding you and connecting you to the nurturing energy of the natural world.

In the distance, you notice a strong and resilient Vine climbing up a trellis. Its tendrils reach out in all directions, symbolizing the Bach Flower Vine remedy, which offers support for cultivating compassion and flexibility in relationships and endeavors.

With each step you take towards the Vine, feel yourself letting go of any feelings of rigidity or dominance that may be weighing you down. Allow yourself to release the grip of control and instead embrace a sense of empathy and understanding.

As you reach the Vine, take a moment to observe its beauty and strength. Notice how it bends and sways with the wind, symbolizing the fluidity and adaptability of life.

Now, imagine yourself sitting beside the Vine, feeling its supportive energy enveloping you. Allow yourself to open your heart to the compassion and flexibility that resides within you, knowing that you are capable of connecting with others with kindness and understanding.

With each breath, breathe in the essence of Vine, allowing its healing energy to wash over you and fill you with a sense of empathy and acceptance. Feel a sense of connection and harmony spreading throughout your entire being, like the intertwining of the Vine's tendrils.

Take a few moments to bask in the nurturing energy of the Vine, knowing that you are always supported and guided towards compassion and flexibility.

When you feel ready, slowly bring your awareness back to the present moment. Wiggle your fingers and toes, gently stretch your body, and take a few more deep breaths.

Know that you can return to this inner sanctuary of compassion and flexibility whenever you need to reconnect with your own inner wisdom.

When you're ready, you can slowly open your eyes and return to the world around you, carrying the sense of openness and kindness with you.

33. Guided Meditation: Embracing Change and Protection with Bach Flower Walnut

Walnut

Find a quiet and comfortable space where you can sit or lie down without any distractions. Close your eyes gently, and take a few deep breaths, allowing yourself to settle into a state of relaxation.

As you continue to breathe deeply, bring your awareness to the center of your chest, the area of your heart. Visualize a soft, warm light glowing in this space, representing the energy of change and protection. Feel this light expanding with each breath, filling your entire being with a sense of resilience and security.

Now, imagine yourself standing in a serene forest, surrounded by towering trees and the gentle rustle of leaves in the breeze. Feel the earth beneath your feet, grounding you and connecting you to the stability of the natural world.

In the distance, you notice a sturdy Walnut tree standing tall and proud. Its branches are adorned with lush green leaves, symbolizing the Bach Flower Walnut remedy, which offers support for navigating transitions and protecting against outside influences.

With each step you take towards the Walnut tree, feel yourself letting go of any feelings of uncertainty or vulnerability that may be weighing you down. Allow yourself to release the grip of fear and instead embrace a sense of strength and resilience.

As you reach the Walnut tree, take a moment to observe its beauty and fortitude. Notice how it stands firm and unwavering, symbolizing the protection and stability that comes from trusting in your own inner wisdom.

Now, imagine yourself sitting beneath the branches of the Walnut tree, feeling its protective energy enveloping you. Allow yourself to open your heart to the change and transformation that resides within you, knowing that you are capable of adapting and growing with grace.

With each breath, breathe in the essence of Walnut, allowing its healing energy to wash over you and fill you with a sense of empowerment and security. Feel a sense of calmness and resilience spreading throughout your entire being, like the sturdy roots of the Walnut tree grounding you to the earth.

Take a few moments to bask in the nurturing energy of the Walnut tree, knowing that you are always supported and guided towards growth and transformation.

When you feel ready, slowly bring your awareness back to the present moment. Wiggle your fingers and toes, gently stretch your body, and take a few more deep breaths.

Know that you can return to this inner sanctuary of change and protection whenever you need to reconnect with your own inner strength.

When you're ready, you can slowly open your eyes and return to the world around you, carrying the sense of resilience and security with you.

34. Guided Meditation: Cultivating Connection and Openness with Bach Flower Water Violet

Water Violet

Find a quiet and comfortable space where you can sit or lie down without any distractions. Close your eyes gently, and take a few deep breaths, allowing yourself to settle into a state of relaxation.

As you continue to breathe deeply, bring your awareness to the center of your chest, the area of your heart. Visualize a soft, warm light glowing in this space, representing the energy of connection and openness. Feel this light expanding with each breath, filling your entire being with a sense of warmth and receptivity.

Now, imagine yourself standing at the edge of a tranquil pond, surrounded by tall reeds and the gentle murmur of water. Feel the earth beneath your feet, grounding you and connecting you to the serenity of the natural world.

In the distance, you notice a cluster of delicate Water Violet flowers floating gracefully on the surface of the pond. These flowers symbolize the Bach Flower Water Violet remedy, which offers support for fostering connection and breaking down barriers.

With each step you take towards the Water Violet flowers, feel yourself letting go of any feelings of aloofness or isolation that may be weighing you down. Allow yourself to release the grip of detachment and instead embrace a sense of belonging and unity.

As you reach the Water Violet flowers, take a moment to observe their beauty and grace. Notice how they dance gently on the water, symbolizing the fluidity and interconnectedness of all beings.

Now, imagine yourself sitting beside the pond, feeling the gentle ripples of the water lapping at your feet. Allow yourself to open your heart to the connection and openness that resides within you, knowing that you are capable of forming deep and meaningful relationships with others.

With each breath, breathe in the essence of Water Violet, allowing its healing energy to wash over you and fill you with a sense of harmony and unity. Feel a sense of peace and acceptance spreading throughout your entire being, like the gentle caress of a summer breeze.

Take a few moments to bask in the nurturing energy of the Water Violet flowers, knowing that you are always supported and connected to the web of life.

When you feel ready, slowly bring your awareness back to the present moment. Wiggle your fingers and toes, gently stretch your body, and take a few more deep breaths.

Know that you can return to this inner sanctuary of connection and openness whenever you need to reconnect with your own inner wisdom.

When you're ready, you can slowly open your eyes and return to the world around you, carrying the sense of unity and belonging with you.

35. Guided Meditation: Cultivating Inner Peace and Mental Clarity with Bach Flower White Chestnut

White Chestnut

Find a quiet and comfortable space where you can sit or lie down without any distractions. Close your eyes gently, and take a few deep breaths, allowing yourself to settle into a state of relaxation.

As you continue to breathe deeply, bring your awareness to the center of your chest, the area of your heart. Visualize a soft, warm light glowing in this space, representing the energy of inner peace and mental clarity. Feel this light expanding with each breath, filling your entire being with a sense of tranquility and focus.

Now, imagine yourself standing in a serene garden, surrounded by lush greenery and the gentle chirping of birds. Feel the earth beneath your feet, grounding you and connecting you to the nurturing energy of nature.

In the distance, you notice a majestic White Chestnut tree standing tall and proud. Its branches are adorned with delicate white flowers, symbolizing the Bach Flower White Chestnut remedy, which offers support for calming a restless mind and finding mental clarity.

With each step you take towards the White Chestnut tree, feel yourself letting go of any racing thoughts or worries that may be occupying your mind. Allow yourself to release the grip of anxiety and instead embrace a sense of peace and stillness.

As you reach the White Chestnut tree, take a moment to observe its beauty and serenity. Notice how it stands firm and unwavering, symbolizing the stability and clarity that comes from quieting the mind.

Now, imagine yourself sitting beneath the branches of the White Chestnut tree, feeling its calming energy enveloping you. Allow yourself to open your mind to the peace and clarity that resides within you, knowing that you are capable of finding stillness amidst the chaos of life.

With each breath, breathe in the essence of White Chestnut, allowing its healing energy to wash over you and fill you with a sense of tranquility and focus. Feel a sense of calmness and mental clarity spreading throughout your entire being, like the gentle rustle of leaves in the wind.

Take a few moments to bask in the nurturing energy of the White Chestnut tree, knowing that you are always supported and guided towards inner peace and mental clarity.

When you feel ready, slowly bring your awareness back to the present moment. Wiggle your fingers and toes, gently stretch your body, and take a few more deep breaths.

Know that you can return to this inner sanctuary of peace and clarity whenever you need to quiet your mind and reconnect with your own inner wisdom.

When you're ready, you can slowly open your eyes and return to the world around you, carrying the sense of tranquility and focus with you.

36. Guided Meditation: Finding Clarity and Purpose with Bach Flower Wild Oat

Wild oat

Find a quiet and comfortable space where you can sit or lie down without any distractions. Close your eyes gently, and take a few deep breaths, allowing yourself to settle into a state of relaxation.

As you continue to breathe deeply, bring your awareness to the center of your chest, the area of your heart. Visualize a soft, warm light glowing in this space, representing the energy of clarity and purpose. Feel this light expanding with each breath, filling your entire being with a sense of direction and focus.

Now, imagine yourself standing in a vast field of wild oats, surrounded by the gentle rustle of the tall grass and the warmth of the sun on your skin. Feel the earth beneath your feet, grounding you and connecting you to the abundance of nature.

In the distance, you notice a single stalk of Wild Oat standing tall and proud amidst the sea of green. Its slender stalk sways gently in the breeze, symbolizing the Bach Flower Wild Oat remedy, which offers support for finding clarity and direction in life's journey.

With each step you take towards the Wild Oat, feel yourself letting go of any feelings of confusion or indecision that may be weighing you down. Allow yourself to release the grip of uncertainty and instead embrace a sense of purpose and determination.

As you reach the Wild Oat, take a moment to observe its beauty and resilience. Notice how it stands firm and unwavering, symbolizing the strength and clarity that comes from knowing your true path.

Now, imagine yourself sitting beside the Wild Oat, feeling its supportive energy enveloping you. Allow yourself to open your heart to the clarity and purpose that resides within you, knowing that you are capable of fulfilling your dreams and aspirations.

With each breath, breathe in the essence of Wild Oat, allowing its healing energy to wash over you and fill you with a sense of direction and focus. Feel a sense of empowerment and determination spreading throughout your entire being, like the gentle sway of the grass in the wind.

Take a few moments to bask in the nurturing energy of the Wild Oat, knowing that you are always supported and guided towards clarity and purpose.

When you feel ready, slowly bring your awareness back to the present moment. Wiggle your fingers and toes, gently stretch your body, and take a few more deep breaths.

Know that you can return to this inner sanctuary of clarity and purpose whenever you need to reconnect with your own inner wisdom.

When you're ready, you can slowly open your eyes and return to the world around you, carrying the sense of direction and focus with you.

37. Guided Meditation: Cultivating Vitality and Engagement with Bach Flower Wild Rose

Wild Rose

Find a quiet and comfortable space where you can sit or lie down without any distractions. Close your eyes gently, and take a few deep breaths, allowing yourself to settle into a state of relaxation.

As you continue to breathe deeply, bring your awareness to the center of your chest, the area of your heart. Visualize a soft, warm light glowing in this space, representing the energy of vitality and engagement. Feel this light expanding with each breath, filling your entire being with a sense of aliveness and enthusiasm.

Now, imagine yourself standing in a vibrant garden, surrounded by colorful flowers and the gentle hum of bees. Feel the earth beneath your feet, grounding you and connecting you to the abundance of life all around you.

In the distance, you notice a single Wild Rose bush standing tall and proud. Its delicate pink petals dance in the breeze, symbolizing the Bach Flower Wild Rose remedy, which offers support for rekindling interest and enthusiasm for life.

With each step you take towards the Wild Rose bush, feel yourself letting go of any feelings of apathy or resignation that may be weighing you down. Allow yourself to release the grip of indifference and instead embrace a sense of joy and engagement.

As you reach the Wild Rose bush, take a moment to observe its beauty and vitality. Notice how it thrives and blooms, symbolizing the possibility of rediscovering passion and purpose in your life.

Now, imagine yourself sitting beside the Wild Rose bush, feeling its vibrant energy enveloping you. Allow yourself to open your heart to the vitality and engagement that resides within you, knowing that you are capable of embracing life with renewed enthusiasm.

With each breath, breathe in the essence of Wild Rose, allowing its healing energy to wash over you and fill you with a sense of aliveness and joy. Feel a sense of excitement and passion spreading throughout your entire being, like the petals of the rose unfolding in the sunlight.

Take a few moments to bask in the nurturing energy of the Wild Rose, knowing that you are always supported and guided towards vitality and engagement.

When you feel ready, slowly bring your awareness back to the present moment. Wiggle your fingers and toes, gently stretch your body, and take a few more deep breaths.

Know that you can return to this inner sanctuary of vitality and engagement whenever you need to reconnect with your own inner passion.

When you're ready, you can slowly open your eyes and return to the world around you, carrying the sense of aliveness and enthusiasm with you.

38. Guided Meditation: Cultivating Acceptance and Resilience with Bach Flower Willow

Willow

Find a quiet and comfortable space where you can sit or lie down without any distractions. Close your eyes gently, and take a few deep breaths, allowing yourself to settle into a state of relaxation.

As you continue to breathe deeply, bring your awareness to the center of your chest, the area of your heart. Visualize a soft, warm light glowing in this space, representing the energy of acceptance and resilience. Feel this light expanding with each breath, filling your entire being with a sense of peace and strength.

Now, imagine yourself standing at the edge of a serene river, surrounded by towering willow trees and the gentle rustle of leaves in the breeze. Feel the earth beneath your feet, grounding you and connecting you to the nurturing energy of nature.

In the distance, you notice a majestic Willow tree standing tall and proud. Its branches sway gracefully in the wind, symbolizing the Bach Flower Willow remedy, which offers support for accepting life's challenges with grace and resilience.

With each step you take towards the Willow tree, feel yourself letting go of any feelings of bitterness or resentment that may be weighing you down. Allow yourself to release the grip of negativity and instead embrace a sense of forgiveness and understanding.

As you reach the Willow tree, take a moment to observe its beauty and strength. Notice how it bends and sways with the wind, symbolizing the flexibility and adaptability of the human spirit.

Now, imagine yourself sitting beneath the branches of the Willow tree, feeling its supportive energy enveloping you. Allow yourself to open your heart to the acceptance and resilience that resides within you, knowing that you are capable of weathering life's storms with grace and dignity.

With each breath, breathe in the essence of Willow, allowing its healing energy to wash over you and fill you with a sense of peace and fortitude. Feel a sense of calmness and strength spreading throughout your entire being, like the gentle rustle of leaves in the wind.

Take a few moments to bask in the nurturing energy of the Willow tree, knowing that you are always supported and guided towards acceptance and resilience.

When you feel ready, slowly bring your awareness back to the present moment. Wiggle your fingers and toes, gently stretch your body, and take a few more deep breaths.

Know that you can return to this inner sanctuary of acceptance and resilience whenever you need to reconnect with your own inner wisdom.

When you're ready, you can slowly open your eyes and return to the world around you, carrying the sense of peace and strength with you.

Conclusion: Embracing Healing and Transformation

As we come to the end of our journey together, we reflect on the profound wisdom and transformative power of Bach Flower remedies and guided meditation practice. Throughout this book, we have explored the essence of each Bach Flower remedy, delving deep into the healing qualities of these remarkable essences and discovering how they can support us on our path to emotional well-being and inner transformation.

Embracing Healing

Bach Flower remedies offer a gentle yet potent means of healing emotional imbalances and restoring harmony to the mind, body, and spirit. Each remedy holds a unique energetic signature that addresses specific emotional states and personality traits, inviting us to explore the depths of our inner landscape and embrace the fullness of our being.

Through guided meditation practice, we have learned to connect with the healing energy of Bach Flower remedies on a deep and transformative level. Guided by the soothing voice of the facilitator, we have journeyed inward, allowing ourselves to release old patterns, cultivate self-awareness, and awaken to the wisdom of our own hearts.

Cultivating Transformation

As we integrate the healing energy of Bach Flower remedies into our lives, we open ourselves to the possibility of profound transformation. We release limiting beliefs, embrace our authentic selves, and step boldly into the fullness of our potential. Guided by the gentle guidance of meditation, we navigate the twists and turns of our inner landscape with grace and ease, knowing that we are supported every step of the way.

Embracing the Journey

The journey of healing and transformation is an ongoing process, one that unfolds with each breath and each moment of awareness. As we continue on our path, may we carry with us the wisdom and insights gained through our exploration of Bach Flower remedies and guided meditation practice. May we remain open to the infinite possibilities that life has to offer and trust in the power of love, compassion, and self-discovery to guide us on our journey.

Gratitude

As we conclude our journey together, we express deep gratitude for the wisdom and guidance of Dr. Edward Bach, whose vision and dedication have brought the healing power of Bach Flower remedies to the world. We also extend our heartfelt thanks to all those who have contributed to this book, sharing their knowledge, insights, and experiences with us along the way.

Closing Reflection

As we close this chapter of our journey, let us take a moment to honor ourselves for the courage and commitment we have shown in embarking on this path of healing and transformation. May we carry the light of love, compassion, and self-awareness with us wherever we go, knowing that we are always supported and guided on our journey back to wholeness.

Thank You

May you Be Well Happy and Peaceful